Documents of American Democracy

MAYFLOWER COMPACT

Christine Honders

New York

Published in 2017 by The Rosen Publishing Group, Inc.
29 East 21st Street, New York, NY 10010

Editor: Katie Kawa
Book Design: Tanya Dellaccio

NOV   '16

Library of Congress Cataloging-in-Publication Data

Names: Honders, Christine, author.
Title: Mayflower Compact / Christine Honders.
Description: New York : PowerKids Press, 2016. | Series: Documents of American democracy | Includes index.
Identifiers: LCCN 2016011881 | ISBN 9781499420852 (pbk.) | ISBN 9781499420876 (library bound) | ISBN 9781499420869 (6 pack)
Subjects: LCSH: Mayflower Compact (1620)–Juvenile literature. | Pilgrims (New Plymouth Colony)–Juvenile literature. | Mayflower (Ship)–Juvenile literature. | Massachusetts–History–New Plymouth, 1620-1691–Juvenile literature.
Classification: LCC F68 .H768 2016 | DDC 974.4/02–dc23
LC record available at http://lccn.loc.gov/2016011881

$19.70

CONTENTS

THE FIRST DOCUMENT OF U.S. GOVERNMENT

Imagine being on a ship for more than two months, sailing toward a land you've never been to or even seen. Think about traveling across the ocean in a cargo ship with no windows and sharing a crowded space with total strangers. Then, imagine that you don't get along with some of the other passengers. It sounds pretty awful, doesn't it?

That's how one of the first groups of **immigrants** came to America in 1620 on a ship called the *Mayflower*. These travelers were from different backgrounds, with different reasons for wanting to travel to the New World. In order to keep the peace, members of the group wrote and signed a document that became known as the Mayflower Compact. It was the first document written by Europeans that established a government in the lands that would become the United States.

The voyage on the Mayflower took 66 days. There were more than 100 people on the ship. The Mayflower Compact was **drafted** to unite these people under one government and set of laws.

The story behind the Mayflower Compact began many years before the *Mayflower* reached the New World. Before 1534, the Catholic religion was the official religion of England. The Roman Catholic Church played a part in the English government. However, when King Henry VIII decided he wanted to divorce his wife, the pope wouldn't allow it. King Henry then decided to break away from the Roman Catholic Church and put himself in charge of his own Church of England.

Some people in England felt the Church of England should be simpler and more pure. These people were called Puritans, and they wanted to work from within the church to make changes. Others—including some of the people who traveled on the *Mayflower*—believed they needed to separate from the Church of England completely.

> *Separatists weren't the same as Puritans. Separatists believed they needed to separate from the Church of England, but Puritans believed they could fix the Church of England while still being part of it.*

SEEKING FREEDOM

*Some people who separated themselves from the Church of England started their own church in Scrooby—a small English village— in the early 1600s. This group and others made their own rules and established their own practices, which angered the leaders of the Church of England. They claimed these people, who became known as Separatists, were breaking laws by ignoring the Church of England's authority. King James I began **persecuting** the Separatists, and they were often treated as traitors. The Separatists either had to worship in secret or leave the country to find religious freedom.*

King James I

In 1608, some of the Separatists traveled to the Netherlands where they'd be free to worship the way they wanted. However, Dutch life was difficult for them. The Separatists had trouble getting jobs that paid well. They also thought Dutch attitudes set a bad example for their children. These Separatists soon decided to travel to the New World.

Separatist leaders signed a contract with the Virginia Company of London to create their own settlement in North America. The Virginia Company was organized by

★ ★ ★ ★ ★ ★ ★ ★ ★ ★ ★ ★ ★ ★ ★ ★

TAKE TWO

The first attempt at the Separatists' journey to the New World ended very quickly. The Speedwell started to leak almost immediately, so that ship and the Mayflower had to turn around. It couldn't be repaired, so some of its passengers crammed themselves onto the Mayflower, which left again on September 6, 1620. Unfortunately, the delay meant the ship was crossing the Atlantic Ocean in the middle of the stormy season. The ship was overcrowded, with 102 passengers on board. Many of them became seasick, making the trip very unpleasant.

King James to settle the east coast of the New World. Some people who didn't share the Separatists' beliefs were gathered to join them. These people wanted to make money in the New World. In August 1620, two ships—the *Speedwell* and the *Mayflower*—began their voyage.

This painting shows the Separatists during a farewell service on the deck of the Speedwell. It was on the back of the U.S. $10,000 bill, which isn't made anymore.

THE *MAYFLOWER* AND ITS PASSENGERS

There were 37 Separatists on the *Mayflower*. Although they organized the trip, they were in the minority. There were fewer Separatists on board than passengers who didn't share their religious beliefs. There was also the crew, which was made up of 20 to 30 men led by the ship's master, Christopher Jones. A master is like a captain.

The *Mayflower* was a cargo ship that was normally used to transport wine and cloth. The cargo was kept in a storage area with no windows under the upper decks. Since the cargo on this trip was the passengers, that's where they stayed. Many crew members stayed in the front of the ship, which was wet and cold from being repeatedly hit by waves. The captain most likely had the driest living area on the ship.

> *One passenger died on the Mayflower's journey. Also, a baby was born during the trip, and he was given the name Oceanus.*

"STRANGERS" AND "SAINTS"

The people on the *Mayflower* were very different. The Separatists were a close-knit group whose main purpose for making this journey was to secure religious freedom. They didn't care about getting rich or starting businesses in the New World. They wanted to start a new religious community. Separatists generally didn't associate with people who didn't share their religious beliefs. They referred to people outside their religion as "strangers." The Separatists also called themselves "saints."

Many "strangers" on this ship had no interest in religious freedom. They wanted money. They believed they would be well paid for this journey, and they hoped there would be more money-making opportunities once they landed in the New World. Some "strangers" were laborers and **indentured servants**.

The Mayflower II *was built to look exactly like the* Mayflower. *You can tour the* Mayflower II *at Plimoth Plantation in Plymouth, Massachusetts, and see just how small the* Mayflower's *living quarters were!*

BECOMING THE PILGRIMS

*The people who traveled on the Mayflower would become known as the Pilgrims, but that wouldn't happen until many years after they settled in the New World. The term "pilgrim" was first found in a piece of writing by a Separatist leader named William Bradford. He called himself and his fellow travelers "pilgrimes" when they left the Netherlands. In 1820, a popular speaker and politician named Daniel Webster referred to the Separatists as "Pilgrim Fathers" during a **bicentennial** celebration of the Mayflower's landing, and the name stuck.*

With such different people together for so many months on the *Mayflower*, there were disagreements. The "strangers" didn't share the Separatists' beliefs, and that caused tension between the two groups. This tension was only made worse by the conditions they faced during the trip. The bad weather made many Pilgrims sick, and they had no other clothes to put on after they got sick. The crew members made fun of them, calling them "puke stockings" and other unkind names.

The travelers were about to face the most **dangerous** situation of their lives. They didn't know what the land or climate would be like, where they'd find food and water, or if they would face hostile native people in the New World. They needed to put their differences aside and work together to survive.

Myles Standish, shown here, was a "stranger" on the Mayflower. *When those who traveled on the* Mayflower *established Plymouth Colony, he became its military leader.*

IMPERFECT LANDING

In early November 1620, the *Mayflower*'s passengers saw land! However, stormy seas had pushed the ship off course, and it was much farther north than it was supposed to be. Instead of being close to the mouth of the Hudson River in present-day New York, it was close to what's now Cape Cod in Massachusetts.

This created a difficult situation. The settlers had no legal right to this new land. Their contract with the Virginia

The Mayflower landed on the tip of Cape Cod in what's now Provincetown, Massachusetts. A group of men began exploring the area for a place to build a colony, and they discovered the future site of Plymouth in December 1620.

Company was no longer in effect because they weren't in the company's **jurisdiction**. Some of the "strangers" argued that, since they weren't in the territory they'd agreed to settle in, they didn't have to follow anyone's orders. They threatened to leave and live on their own. The Separatists, however, knew that the colony would fall apart without formal laws.

MAKING A PACT

Even though the idea of total freedom must have been tempting for the "strangers," they eventually agreed with the Separatists that it would be better for all of them if some order was established. The settlers needed to make a compact, or an agreement, with each other that they would all follow.

The Separatists began drafting this compact before they even left the *Mayflower*. William Brewster, who was a Separatist with a college education, was one of its main authors, along with William Bradford, who eventually served as governor of Plymouth Colony. What we now call the Mayflower Compact is purposely short—about 200 words. It laid the foundation for self-government, and it served as an agreement that the settlers would live and work together under the same laws.

*William Brewster was a Separatist who was an elder member of the Scrooby **congregation**. While in the Netherlands, he printed religious **pamphlets**, such as the one shown here. He then illegally sent the pamphlets to England. Once settled in the New World, Brewster became the religious leader of Plymouth Colony.*

WILLIAM BREWSTER

THE "BODY POLITIC"

The Mayflower Compact isn't a constitution. It's been described by many as a social contract. William Bradford called it "an association and agreement." This agreement was binding, meaning it couldn't be broken, and it states that the settlers would form a "civil body politic," or a group that would create a government. The group chose its leaders through a majority vote. The laws they would establish would be "for the general good of the Colony."

Because the Mayflower Compact was written by Separatists, it looks similar to the agreements their religious groups wrote when starting new churches. The Separatists took this model and applied it to the establishment of a government for ordinary citizens. This document is the first recorded step toward creating a democratic government in what's now the United States.

The Mayflower Compact was signed by 41 men—nearly all the male passengers on the ship.

SIGNING ON THE SHIP

The Mayflower Compact was signed on the Mayflower on November 11, 1620. The passengers spent nearly the entire winter on the Mayflower. Plymouth Colony was established in December 1620, but the passengers continued to live on the ship while they built their homes. The settlers weren't used to the harsh weather in this part of the world, and nearly half of them died that winter from sickness and a lack of food.

"Having undertaken, for the glory of God, and advancement of the Christian faith, and honor of our King and Country, a voyage to plant the first colony in the northern parts of Virginia, do by these presents solemnly and mutually, in the presence of God, and one of another, covenant and combine our selves together into a civil body politic, for our better ordering and preservation and furtherance of the ends aforesaid...."

The Mayflower Compact isn't a declaration of independence. In fact, in the beginning of the document, the settlers declare their loyalty to King James of England. However, it did influence the Founding Fathers when they wrote the U.S. Constitution after becoming independent from England.

One of the most important concepts in the Mayflower Compact is the idea that "just and equal laws" would be made for the people, by the people. The Mayflower Compact is an agreement acknowledging that, as a group, the settlers would work together for survival. They knew those "just and equal laws" would help them survive. The signers of the Mayflower Compact established majority rule as the way they would approve these laws and vote for leaders.

The original Mayflower Compact has been lost. This handwritten copy by William Bradford was found in his journal, which was later published as Of Plymouth Plantation.

establishes importance of religion

considered themselves in the northern part of the Virginia colony

states loyalty to English king

"civil body politic"

date signed: November 11

year signed: 1620

"just and equal laws"

THE FIRST ELECTION

Almost immediately after signing the Mayflower Compact, its signers elected their first governor. They elected John Carver. He was a Separatist and a businessman who helped make the deal with the Virginia Company to finance the trip on the *Mayflower*. Carver was one of the signers of the Mayflower Compact, and he helped discover the land where Plymouth Colony would be built.

Carver's most important accomplishment was the peace treaty he made with the Wampanoag people. In April 1621, less than a year after he was elected governor, Carver died.

In June 1621, members of Plymouth Colony received a new **patent** from England, giving them rights to the land. The Mayflower Compact was no longer needed. However, its influence remained.

NATIVE AMERICAN NEIGHBORS

The Pilgrims mainly interacted with a Wampanoag leader named Ousamequin. However, because the Wampanoag people called each of their leaders a Massasoit, the Pilgrims mistakenly believed Ousamequin's first name was Massasoit. The relationship between the Pilgrims and Wampanoag people was generally friendly. The Pilgrims even wrote of a harvest celebration they shared with members of the Wampanoag community. This is often considered the first Thanksgiving.

This painting of the Pilgrims and Wampanoag people shows their friendly relationship.

Although the Mayflower Compact was no longer in effect, it influenced the democratic policies adopted by the colonists. Freemen, or the adult men of the colony, were the only ones allowed to vote. However, the privilege of voting came with responsibility, and freemen were fined if they didn't attend General Court, which had both legislative and judicial **roles** in the colony.

As the population grew and the colony expanded into multiple settlements, it became impossible for all the freemen to attend meetings of the General Court. By 1638, separate settlements were allowed to have their own meetings and then choose a representative to send to most General Court meetings.

William Bradford also worked with Edward Winslow to write Mourt's Relation, *which is a journal of the* Mayflower *trip and the Pilgrims' early days in Plymouth Colony.* Mourt's Relation *contains what's believed to be one of the first copies of the Mayflower Compact.*

WILLIAM BRADFORD

After the sudden death of John Carver in April 1621, William Bradford was elected governor of Plymouth Colony. He was a Separatist who'd traveled to the Netherlands and then helped organize the Mayflower trip. He was also one of the main authors of the Mayflower Compact. Bradford was reelected governor 30 times between 1621 and 1656. His personal writings about the Mayflower voyage and the settlement of Plymouth Colony have helped us learn what life was like for the Pilgrims.

The Mayflower Compact wasn't the only contribution the members of Plymouth Colony made to the establishment of American government as we know it today. In 1636, the General Court created a legal code for the colony. This was the first legal code in what would become the United States. This code also contains what some historians consider to be a bill of rights, which included the right to a trial by jury. This right is an important part of a democratic society, and it's one of the foundations of the American legal system.

Plymouth Colony never got a royal **charter** from the English king. Instead, in 1691, this colony became part of the much larger Massachusetts Bay Colony.

PLYMOUTH ROCK

1608	*Some Separatists travel to the Netherlands.*
August 1620	*The Mayflower and the Speedwell depart for the New World, but both ships turn back when the leaky Speedwell is forced to to stay in England.*
September 6, 1620	*The Mayflower voyage officially begins.*
November 11, 1620	*The Mayflower Compact is written and signed. John Carver is elected governor.*
December 1620	*Plymouth Colony is established.*
April 1621	*Carver dies suddenly, and William Bradford is elected governor.*
June 1621	*Plymouth Colony receives a new patent from England. The Mayflower Compact is no longer needed.*
1638	*The General Court of Plymouth allows freemen at other settlements to meet and select representatives to attend meetings.*
1691	*Plymouth Colony becomes part of the Massachusetts Bay Colony.*

Plymouth Colony only existed for 71 years. In that time, its founders left their mark on the future of American democracy.

Even though the Mayflower Compact hadn't been needed for more than a century by the time Americans declared their independence from England in 1776, it had a major influence on what would become modern American democracy. Its definition of a "civil body politic" and its framework for self-government are concepts that can be seen in the U.S. Constitution. Its signers established a majority-rule voting system that's reflected in the American political process today. It also highlighted the importance of creating a government that worked for the good of the people, which is exactly what the U.S. government is supposed to do.

The Mayflower Compact is an agreement written and signed as a means of survival for some of the first American colonists. It also laid the foundation for a new democracy.

GLOSSARY

bicentennial: A 200th anniversary or its celebration.

charter: A document issued by a government that gives rights to a person or group.

congregation: A religious community.

dangerous: Not safe.

draft: To put something into written form.

immigrant: A person who comes to a country to live there.

indentured servant: A person who is bound to work for another for a specific period of time, often in exchange for passage to a new country.

jurisdiction: The limits or territory within which a person or group can exercise authority.

pamphlet: A short printed publication with no cover or with a paper cover.

patent: An official land grant.

persecute: To treat a person or group of people cruelly or unfairly, especially because of race or religious or political beliefs.

role: A part or function.

INDEX

WEBSITES

Due to the changing nature of Internet links, PowerKids Press has developed an online list of websites related to the subject of this book. This site is updated regularly. Please use this link to access the list:

www.powerkidslinks.com/amdoc/maycom